2

A **Sunday** in Purgatory

A Sunday in **Purgatory**

ACKNOWLEDGMENTS

"A Terrific Headache" and "A Sunday in Purgatory" were published in *Nimrod International Journal*, Issue 57, Spring/Summer 2013.

"Legacy," "Eventide," "Ladyfingers" and "A Half Open Door" were published in *Passager*, in 2013, 2014, 2015, and 2016, respectively.

A Sunday in Purgatory

Copyright © 2016 Henry Morgenthau III
All rights reserved
First Edition 2016
Published in the United States of America
Printed by Spencer Printing
ISBN 978-0-9969726-4-2

Publisher's Cataloging-In-Publication Data
(Prepared by The Donohue Group, Inc.)

Names: Morgenthau, Henry, 1917-
Title: A Sunday in purgatory / Henry Morgenthau III.
Description: First edition. | Baltimore, MD : Passager Books, 2016.
Identifiers: ISBN 978-0-9969726-4-2
Subjects: LCSH: Old age--Poetry. | Families--Poetry. | Love--Poetry. | Death--Poetry. |
American poetry.
Classification: LCC PS3613.O74 S86 2016 | DDC 811/.6--dc23

Passager Books is in residence in the Klein Family School
of Communications Design at the University of Baltimore.

Passager Books
1420 North Charles Street
Baltimore, Maryland 21201
www.passagerbooks.com

A Sunday in Purgatory

HENRY MORGENTHAU III

Passager Books
Baltimore, MD
2016

CONTENTS

To Ruth
and our children,
Sarah, Ben and Kramer
and our grandchildren

And David Keplinger,
Bonnie Naradzay
and Robert Nover

And to all my Ingleside friends

Desire, desire, desire.
The longing for the dance
stirs in the buried life.

from "Touch Me" by STANLEY KUNITZ

AUTHOR'S NOTE

Writing poetry for me is a celebration of the evening of a long life, a coda, a strikingly new expression of my inner being that surprises me as much as those who know me. Now as death kindly waits for me, I am enlivened with thoughts I can't take with me.

In my delayed vocation I have found solace and inspiration in the example of Stanley Kunitz, who continued to write and to tend his garden until the year before he died at one hundred. In one of his last poems, he wrote, "I can scarcely wait 'til tomorrow when a new life begins for me, as it does each day."

But the poet who inspired me the most, as I began to write poems, was Robert Lowell. Kunitz had written that Lowell's *Life Studies* was perhaps the most influential book for modern poetry since Eliot's, *The Wasteland*.

Earlier in my career as a public television producer and writer in Boston, I met with Lowell a number of times, both in his New York apartment and in Castine, Maine, with him and his wife Elizabeth Hardwick, to discuss the possibility of making a documentary film, using excerpts of *Life Studies.*

My visit was a rare opportunity to observe the intensely disciplined routine of a poet at work. Each morning Lowell isolated himself in a fisherman's shack. What the poet, Mary Oliver, calls "a patch of profound unbroken solitude." Then after a short break for a tuna fish sandwich lunch, back to work until late afternoon Martinis. Ultimately Lowell decided he would be willing to have us record him reading his poems, but not to allow a documentary film.

In a letter dated July 29, 1964, following my Castine visit, he wrote:

> "What is needed, I think, is for me to appear as a poet, mind and imagination, rather than as a story . . . I think I would begin to wander if I were real or merely an eye floating outside its body and existence."

Lowell's confessional poems continue to serve as a guiding light to illuminate my own poetry. In these precious days I dress my private demons in these scribblings to come out from behind the shadows that have darkened my long and privileged life, sometimes choking, sometimes joking, in a purgatory where I wait to pass through the open gates.

Henry Morgenthau

A Sunday in Purgatory

YOU'LL CATCH YOUR DEATH

"You'll catch your death of cold," Mother would say
if I went outside without my jacket, cap and mittens.
When I was older, plagued with an infected tooth,
the dentist numbed my nerve with Laughing Gas.
I felt the pain from his drilling but laughed as if

it were hurting someone else, not me.
Then, at Deerfield, my best friend swallowed
a corrosive base in chemistry lab to end his life,
but recovered to graduate. Next year at Dartmouth,
he lay down across the tracks to wait for the train.

Now death has begun to catch up with me.
I've lived too long. Merely standing up
and breathing in and out is a serious challenge.
At Ingleside, our retirement home, we progress
from canes, to walkers, to wheelchairs.

In vain we try to push back looming shadows
as frequent announcements of memorial services
are posted where they can't be missed:
advertisements luring us to that final vacation.

LADYFINGERS

In our apartment
on Manhattan's Upper West Side,
a safe haven for prosperous German Jews,
I was cushioned by my loving mother
who assured me I would grow up to be
anything I wanted to be,
even as my father's anger spilled over me
like vitriol. He had his own problems,
trying to fulfill his immigrant father's dreams.

When the time came
to step out of my cocoon,
I discovered a world
where Mother couldn't protect me.
My first adventures were staged
a few blocks uptown
at the Birch Wathen kindergarten.
On the first day of classes,
boys and girls were separated.
The girls were handed
pastel-colored chiffon scarves
to wave as they gamboled about.
I grabbed one, and followed the girls,

prompting jeers from the boys.
"Hey Ladyfingers," yelled Henry Furnald,
the best looking boy in the class.
"Hey Ladyfingers!"
He was one of the boys. I was not.

During the many years
from my uneasy childhood to old age,
I have lived with the dread of being
uncovered. I have built walls
to isolate myself, to hide behind,
to fear, and to hate myself.
Walls fabricated with stony
indifference toward being different.

Not wanting to be touched.
Wanting to touch.
Wanting to be caressed by the soft,
sensuous pressure of warm bath water.
I shiver as I step out
in my exposed nakedness.

LIVING EFFIGY

My dear departed Cousin Howard,
was it as a kindred spirit you approached me
at my grandmother's funeral? Like me, you were
a non-entity in your own right, the older brother
of a prominent younger brother, in whose shadow
you could never comfortably disappear.
You barked like an old dog, trying to clear
your throat, stuck with something
you could never quite break through.

In my freshman year at Princeton,
I was a lonely kid
born and brought up in New York City.
My parents had just moved to Washington,
to blossom in The New Deal.

On weekends, I stayed with my grandmother
at her apartment in the Savoy Plaza Hotel
on 59th and Fifth Avenue. You were a recluse,
living four blocks south in high style
at the elegant St. Regis. After Grandma died,
you invited me to be your guest
whenever I returned. I accepted.

My parents were poor relations
in an extended family that had prospered
exponentially during the Roaring Twenties.

Then, when the nation sank into the depths
of the Depression, ruined Wall Street brokers
were jumping out of their office windows.
Yet there seemed no need to rein in your ways.
You, my dear cousin, were floating through life
on inherited wealth, a very odd duck.

1920 was the final year of the flu epidemic.
The scourge that spared no one,
leveled the privileged with the poor,
and decimated the veterans of the War
to end all wars. It stole your beloved wife.
She died delivering your stillborn son.
I don't believe you ever again pressed your flesh
against flesh. When occasionally you ventured
out of your lair, you wore gloves as protection
against a threatening handshake.

I remember your so-called theater parties.
We guests ate dinner in your quarters,
catered by room service.
Following our cloistered feast,
you dispatched us to occupy choice seats
at a popular Broadway show
while you remained at home.

After the final curtain fell, we were picked up
by the chauffer-driven limousine, a bequest
from your father-in-law, Willie Walter,
the body specially designed
so that he could enter his carriage
without stooping. The festive evening
ended when we rejoined you
for a brandy in your library,
lined with your collection of incunabula.

I often wonder why you singled me out
for such lavish favors.
Could it be you saw in me the living effigy
of the man your son might have grown up to be?

A MARVELOUS PARTY

At Cap d'Antibes, summer of 1938,
Beatrice Lillie's son, Bobby Peel,
becomes my brother Bob's chum.
For the future heroes and collaborationists
basking together in the Mediterranean sun,
it is "our last summer."

I listen to that cheeky chanteuse,
Bea (Lady Peel), hair trimmed short
like a man's, long before it was the fashion.
Wispy voice is without a wisp of sadness.

She sings of a marvelous party. Enter Lulu:
You would never have guessed
from her fisherman's vest,
that her bust had been whittled away.
I couldn't have loved it more.

Four years later, while entertaining
British troops, Bea received notice her son,
serving in the Navy, had died at sea.
Old trooper that she was,
Bea performed that night.
"I'll cry tomorrow," she said.

NET WORTHINESS

Pack up your troubles
in your old kit bag,
and hand them over
to your psychiatrist.

You can't buy solutions.
But if you pay him enough
to help find your lost marbles
it will feel like money well spent.

The problem is that this
could burst the bubble
of your net worthiness
leaving you worthless.

HELP!

"You're old enough, my son, your shoes to tie,"
my loving mother told me. I was four.
I thought, with her to tie them, need I try?
I told myself her wishes I'd ignore.

Designed a template for a passive life
devoid of all ambition's strain and stress,
I gladly ceded to my loving wife,
who saw no limits to a gal's success.

But now with more than ninety years behind,
of mother and my dearest wife bereft,
alas my shoes untied again I find.
But in these precious years I've no strength left.

A TERRIFIC HEADACHE

Anna brought Lucy to the White House
when Eleanor was on the road.
This father and daughter conspiracy
was a family secret.
Others in the know were committed to silence.
My parents knew. They never told me.

My father was visiting the President
for dinner at Warm Springs.
Before that last supper, he steadied
the trembling hand
of his long time boss and friend
as he mixed Bourbon Old Fashioneds and nibbled
caviar, a gift from the Soviet ambassador.
Four ladies were his guests.

Cousin Laura Delano, with her dog.
She had never married, her gray, deeply blued
coiffure sported a shaved widow's peak.
Daisy Suckley, Hyde Park neighbor,
and more, gossip would have it.
And then there was Lucy Mercer Rutherford,
slipped over from her Aiken estate

with artist, Mme. Shoumatoff.
Lucy had commissioned a private portrait
of her beloved.

The next afternoon Laura called Eleanor
at the White House. Franklin had fainted
and was carried to his bed. She was not to be
alarmed. To prevent rumors from flying,
she kept her date to speak to the ladies
at the Sulgrave Club.

Summoned to the phone by the press secretary
Steve Early, Eleanor later wrote,
"He asked me to come home at once.
I did not even ask why.
I knew in my heart of hearts what had happened."

That night Laura told Eleanor
in her absence Lucy had come for dinner
at the White House on several occasions
with Eleanor's daughter Anna serving as hostess.

Eleanor's bitterness and sadness remained private:
"He might have been happier with a wife

who was completely uncritical," she wrote.
"He had to find it in some other people.
I was one of those who served his purposes."

On that final day in the Little White House
in Warm Springs, insulated
from the cries of war,
the Commander in Chief, posing
in his favorite Navy cape,
put his hand to his temple.
His last words, "I have a terrific headache."

EVENTIDE

Trying to live on time that I borrow,
coasting downhill on a one-way street.
Here today, I fear tomorrow
when there'll be nothing I'll know how to say.
Words once at tongue's tip now seem out of reach.
No more dressing naked images in rhymes,
fabricating gowns of modesty from old songs.
The day is over, light is fading fast.
It is time to go and stay
where there is no time, no space,
no shadow to escape from or chase.
A blind pilgrim, I stumble unseeing
in a search for God.

BEHIND THE SHADOW

Behind the shadow of myself,
forgotten but not gone,
the secret I dared not expose,
I kept while life went on.

I fear, dear one, it's now too late.
No need the lie deny.
The truth became irrelevant,
so why reveal the lie?

FOR SHAME

I need to be the person
my friends and family believe me to be.
I can't be the person I am,
but can't push him out.
I fear him, he is strangling me.
Perhaps he will be stillborn
after I die, if you know what I mean.

FORGIVE ME

Daddy, you look right through me,
failing to stop on the way
to see what's inside.
That's what we all do.
Yoo-hoo, yes you, Daddy,
I don't know who you are.
I prefer to see you from afar.
Are you trying to be close to me?
Daddy, I don't know why or
what you want to see,
outside or inside me.
Is it forgiveness you ask?
Or forgiveness I must seek?

THE HALF OPEN DOOR

While listening to the moaning
of a ghostly choir of lost lovers,
I try to tell you the truth,
half hoping you don't hear me,
as I desperately try to expel
something stuck in my soul
I can't bear to live with,
but don't want to die with.

With a furtive sideways glance
I peer through a half open door, to behold
a body gnarled like an old cherry tree.
Exposed shaft at half-mast,
he stands between an iconic David,
beautiful in his awkward adolescent grace,
and a redolent overripe Schiele harlot.

As though in a pas de deux,
he moves as I move.
Is he my partner or my mirror image?
When the mirror shatters, the truth will out,
with half truth seen through a door half open.

THE UNBUTTONED SHIRT

A mystery is what
you don't want to know
about the people you know.
What he wanted me to know
when he unbuttoned his shirt.
I wish I'd known then
what I know now.

HELLO EVERYBODY, HELLO, HELLO

Kin and kith, kindred spirits all,
gathered here to greet each other cheerfully,
and to cheer me over a big bump in the road.

A long road traveled so many
more years than I counted on.
If you are listening, please don't count on
words of wisdom from this ancient mariner
with shattered and distorted vision,
thanks to macular degeneration.

Looking down the road I see the future dimly,
as through a spattered windshield,
its frozen wiper unyielding.

But not to complain,
the rose tinted rear-view mirror
revives a carefully edited past,
when all of us adolescents were above average,
with parents – your grand or great-grandparents –
struggling to make real a New Deal for all.

BEFORE THE CLOSING BELL

I'm trying to write a villanelle,
but nothing seems to come to mind,
no inspiration before the closing bell.

Online I seek verses some poet will sell –
a prostitute of the literary kind –
to help cobble together a villanelle.

I looked to Milton, returned from hell,
his vision sharpened when he went blind,
he gave no inspiration before the closing bell,

nor can Dante or Virgil help break the spell.
I'm destined forever to be caught in a bind,
the guy who couldn't write a villanelle,

no second chance to break out of my shell.
The end looms in sight, darkly defined.
God, bless me, before sounding the closing bell.

There is no hereafter, no heaven, no hell,
but I search for a poem to leave behind.
Still trying to write a villanelle,
I pray for inspiration before the closing bell.

BURNT TOAST

Afraid to love, I make love
to the beloved of another,
never daring to come out,

I live under anonymous cover.
In a dark room I spy on life
through a shattered window.

To intimates, to those who would love me,
there are secrets I cannot bear to share
that I confess to strangers, happily.

I look for diamonds buried in the sand.
I find instead, a rusted knife. A slap
in the face greets my extended hand.

My fingers blistered by a vengeful stove,
I scrape bitter crumbs from burnt toast,
to taste the kiss I miss the most.

CRÊPE DE CHINE

Slouched in unraveling rattan chairs,
Mother's ghost between the two of us,
in the sunset's haunting afterglow

I ask my brother –
Can it be that we grizzled codgers
are more provocative,
clothed in multicolored
deception rather than exposed
in our honest nakedness,

stripped of comfortable old lies
that over many decades
have crusted tears, and

warped our bodies,
our bones barely
covered by skin,

dried thin and wrinkled,
like the crêpe de chine of
Mother's faded evening gown?

ODE

O Mother, life for you was much too short
for me alas too long the years to grieve,
once cherished memories fading I contort.
Those haunting shadows now my sole reprieve.
A family blood disease stole you away.
You hid from us your sharpened bitter pains.
You sang for us those songs with sweet refrains,
a legacy for us that's here to stay.
You had no time to realize golden dreams
that died with you alone, or so it seems.

DANSE MACABRE

While tumbling out of an interrupted nightmare,
body parts, like shards of vertebrae
strung together on a limp clothesline,
a spinal cord wriggling its way at midnight,
snakes down a deserted hallway,
dancing to the discordant music
of irregular breathing,
punctuated with loud snorts,
kept in check behind the face mask
of my sleep apnea machine.
The pacemaker implanted in my chest
is an unyielding metronome
synchronizing disobedient heartbeats.

Oh yes, I almost forgot – I do forget
more often than I can remember –
to tell you why
I remember that deserted hallway:
It's the backbone that supports
the heavy burden of walk-in closets
designed for independent living residents,
living on time borrowed at exorbitant interest rates.

In our ever shortening waking hours,
punctuated by extensive naps,
we link our spindly arms to dance,
thirsting for one more cup of kindness yet.

LATE

At ninety-eight,
I hate being late.
Too late to date
Too late to mate
Too late to die?

They will recall
that day in the fall
that old so-and-so
found time to go.

LEGACY

In a sturdy mahogany cabinet
on display behind locked glass doors,
I secure Grandma's fragile Limoges china
and sparkling Waterford cut crystal.
Mother's jewelry, Grandpa's solid gold pocket watch
and a set of monogrammed flat silver for eighteen,
are stored inconveniently in a bank vault.
Collected works of art, insured at two percent a year,
will be repurchased twice in half a century.
And so, too constipated to gain relief
with gifts to patiently waiting heirs,
I struggle to survive, possessed by my possessions.

FOGGY BOTTOM NIGHT

On an outing from my neglected grave,
stumbling in the soupy dense darkness
of a July Foggy Bottom night,
disjointed skeleton clothed in wrinkled skin.

I penetrate the sealed door
of your celibate chamber
dimly illuminated by moonbeams

filtered through a filthy skylight,
black walls mounted with
decapitated heads of scalped lovers.

My eyeless gaze falls on your naked body
of sculpted tarnished silver,
asleep on an unmade bed.
I sniff the acrid stench of unwashed armpits.

Our dreams pass like ships sailing
on the ocean of my pluperfect years
and of your years yet to come.

Fuck you my friend. I only asked for
one night's sojourn above the ground.

NO FUTURE, NO PAST

It starts with the word that's
hiding somewhere from my tongue,
very annoyingly not forthcoming.

Leaves me feeling quite unstrung.
Give me a break – there's a lot at stake,
hiding somewhere from my tongue.

I think I found it! What do you know.
Thanks for the break;
there's a lot at stake.

But now I'm in deep trouble, better go slow.
I can't remember what I can't remember.
Lost forever, what do you know.

Perhaps it's the freedom that comes
in December. I can't remember
what I can't remember.

There is no future, there is no past.
It starts with the word that labels something,
very annoyingly not forthcoming.

WOW

At ninety-nine
I can't say I have had
everything I expected out of life,
but I have had about all I want.
These days my family and good friends
are relentless cheerleaders.
Their cheers I can do without.
They look me over and say, "Wow!"
I yell, "Ow!!"

SCRAPS OF YESTERDAYS

It was one of those crazy days –
artificial moments in the game of life –
when there is no time.
Time out from now
for a sentimental journey to then,
where we visit our dead,
reveling in scraps of yesterdays
glued together in a collage
like our dreams.
A cocktail party
for guests from everywhere,
arriving just in time.

SENTENCED FOR LIFE

I hate being told what to do,
but love being told what to do, too.
With my progressive school classmates I'd say
"Do we have to do what we want to do today?"
Now, years later, I go to my rabbi, Ben Zion Gold,
pleading to be told what to do, what choices to make.

An Auschwitz survivor,
once stripped of power to make any decisions
except to hasten death with a senseless act
of defiance, he feels guilty
to be alive. He tells me,
"Do whatever pleases you."
That's a big help.

Faced with the curse of infinite choices,
am I unknowingly cruel, seeking help
from one whose black memories
are a life sentence,
never to be pardoned?

SERIOUS CRIMES

If someone uses a word
he doesn't understand,
that's a misdemeanor.
If he grabs onto words
he doesn't understand at all,
that's a felony.
But when someone uses words
totally unknown to most of us,
let him stew in his own juiciness.
Still it is always a pardonable crime
if it provides an artful rhyme.

SHIP OF FOOLS

Hey, I'm here to stay –
for a little while, anyway.
To take orders, to give orders
to the help, who are paid
to help the helpless.

Caretakers, who don't care
that our stumbling is humbling,
we who radiate the foul smell of old age.
The odor of rage rattles the cage
of our purgatory, out of loved ones' way,

aboard a ship of fools where we can stay.
At the final port of call,
someone will meet us
with a living will.

THE LAST ACT

I'm telling you my dear,
dying is the most important
event in your life.
You can rehearse it
in your head and with your body.
You can prepare for it
all your life,
you can only do it once,
there is no looking back.
You can never ask,
"Did I do it well?"
You will never know.
No one will know.
It will be said,
"Surrounded by his loving family,
he died peacefully."
Cold comfort for the warm-blooded:
a sugar-coated lie.

YES, VIRGINIA, THERE IS A GOD

Not the God worshiped by your parents
nor those who appear to love or despise you.
Not the God we created to guide us
on that short journey called life,
a journey on a narrow bumpy road.
Not the God that empowers us
with shock absorbers to travel ever faster
from generation to generation,
more comfortably, more hazardously,
as we try to reach out beyond the world
designed for us. A world where all humans
are created unequal.
Not the God who masquerades as our shepherd,
grades our talents, foresees our destiny.
Not the God who protects us against our enemies,
who have made deals with their own gods.
Not the God who resides in a holy place
and hears our prayers.

So, Virginia,
may you grow up to discover
the God you can never hear nor speak to,
who dwells in sacred space.

THE MAN IN THE DOUBLE-BREASTED SUIT

I met with him in Boston's genteel St. Botolph Club.
Benjamin Welles, *New York Times* correspondent,
was a rumpled version of Sumner Welles, his father,
who was elegant and even fastidious
in his Savile Row bespoke double-breasted suits.

To unburden himself of his father's double life,
Welles struggled to write a long postponed biography.
In the dimly lit lounge, we drank our whiskey,
served on porcelain plates that once served as ballast
in the hold of a clippership bound from China.

Mellowing as the evening darkened, we were sons
of two close friends of Franklin Roosevelt,
who appointed them to high ranks during the New Deal.
Sumner Welles, Under Secretary of State, and my father
were both on board the President's train that night,

returning, with Roosevelt and his retinue, to Union Station
after attending the funeral of the Speaker of the House,
William Bankhead, in his home town in Alabama.
Sitting in the dining car, Sumner persuaded colleagues
to drink with him. By four a.m., alone in the dining car,

he barely managed to stagger back to his stateroom
and summon a porter for coffee. This proud black man
discovered that Sumner, sitting naked on his berth,
had desires other than coffee. Later, he summoned
two more porters with the same requests.

Privy to these events were only the Secret Service agents,
who reported directly to my father, the Treasury Secretary.
After my father died, I read cryptic notes in his diaries
that tied the story together. He asked all in the know
to remain silent. But no secret remains buried forever.

William Bullitt acquired the damning evidence.
He too was a diplomat, the first U.S. Ambassador
to the Soviet Union, then Ambassador to France
in World War II. This Iago, bearing affidavits, leaked
the tale, forcing Roosevelt to accept Welles' resignation.

But when Bullitt came to the White House, Roosevelt
went white with rage. "What Welles may have done
is between him and his God," he said. "But what you
have done to destroy another man is unpardonable.
You may go straight to Hell."

The St. Botolph lounge had long since emptied. Rising to bid me good night, Benjamin resumed his courtly posture. His *Sumner Welles: FDR's Global Strategist*, when it came out, was well received, but no bestseller. One reviewer called it "painfully candid."

ECHOES

I look for words that bounce off each other,
singing a song of unspeakable thoughts
that seduces and strangles, caught
by a cool unpredictable breeze
that plays the sad music of trees' rustling leaves.
A breeze that makes branches
sway back and forth, back and forth.
Nature's ballet that repeats its symmetry
more or less, but never exactly the same,
like Mozart, failing to tame his inspired
temptation, for yet another variation,
unlike Haydn's exact repetition,
he composed music by the meter
to delight the Esterhazys,
but was deaf to the haunting rhythm,
the swing of an invisible pendulum
swaying back and forth, back and forth.
A relentless foreboding that there'll be
a time when no time is left for anything,
but time for the stillness of nothing.
I hear the echoes of a poet's refrain, caught
singing a song of unspeakable thoughts.

UNSIGHTLY IMAGE

You may bring me lunch on a tray.
Just leave it. Don't stay.
I don't want to see you.
What I really mean is
I don't want you to see me.

Unexpectedly I caught sight
of an old guy the other day,
in a mirror. A crippled derelict
stumbling forward
in a slow syncopated hobble.
I tried to turn away from
that unsightly image of myself.

You may bring me lunch on a tray.

UPENDED

Can the unseen
be obscene?
Can bad taste
be tasted?
Is a misfit
unfit?
Hurrying to get there,
what is there?

If you think you will slip,
don't take a trip.
Stay home, take another sip.
If life could extend
with no foreseeable end,
let boredom spirit you
around the bend.

VIRTUAL

Reaching out to you, we're representing
gods and demigods that you've invented.
We're trying to inform you we're unhappy
with treatment of the world we gave you.
We asked for little more than your respect.
Take heed! You can reach us at our new blog
4godssakehighheavenandhell.org
We are at war against each other's brothers
to conquer hearts and minds and souls
and all the land that you have tried to hold.
You sought to gain our favor with your gold,
trusted then our paper, then our plastic.
Now with Bitcoin we've turned virtual.
You may find your true God without ritual.

OUR CROWD

I grew up in the gilded ghetto
of Manhattan's Upper West Side,
the choice sites on and just off
Central Park West; it extended westward,
way out west on West End Avenue.

My forebears had voyaged to these shores,
not to escape deadly oppression, not in chains,
but lured by tales of golden opportunities.
Immigrant great-grandparents and grandparents,
transplanted in the burgeoning cities
of their new homeland,
sank deep roots and prospered
in tandem with Christian neighbors,
almost equal but separate.
For us there were two kinds of people,
Jews and non-Jews. To this day,
if you are a non-Jew, you can't tell Jewish jokes,
at least not to Jews.

During the normalcy of the Roaring Twenties,
my family began swimming
into the mainstream, carefully.

If a non-Jew said "Jew,"
with good intentions, or no intentions,
it bore the sting of anti-Semitism.
We shielded ourselves with euphemisms.
Rabbi Stephen Wise spoke of "our people."
For my Aunt Hattie it was "Our Crowd."

Presiding over his lavish Sunday dinner table,
my great-uncle Arthur Lehman,
senior partner at Lehman Brothers,
always whispered when he said "Jew."
"Why are you whispering?" asked his daughter, Frances
– she was called Peter, he had hoped for a son –
"we are all Jews here, aren't we?"

A SUNDAY IN PURGATORY

A voluntary inmate immured
in a last resort for seniors,
there are constant reminders,
the reaper is lurking around that corner.
I am at home, very much at home,
here at Ingleside at Rock Creek.
Distant three miles from my caring daughter.

At Ingleside, a faith-based community
for vintage Presbyterians, I am an old Jew.
But that's another story.
I'm not complaining with so much I want to do,
doing it at my pace, slowly.
Anticipation of death is like looking for a new job.

Then suddenly on a Sunday,
talking recklessly while eating brunch,
a gristly piece of meat lodges in my throat.
I struggle for breath, too annoyed to be scared.
Someone pounds my back to no avail.
Out of nowhere, an alert pint-sized waiter
performs the Heimlich maneuver.
I don't believe it will work.
It does! Uncorked, I am freed.

Looking up I see the concerned visage and
reversed collar of a retired Navy chaplain,
pinch hitting as God's messenger for the day.
Had he come to perform the last rites,
to ease my passage from this world to the hereafter?
Don't jump to dark conclusions.
In World War II on active duty,
he learned the Heimlich as well as the *himmlisch*.
Knowing it is best administered
to a standing victim,
he rushed to intervene.
On this day I am twice blessed
with the kindness of strangers.

ENVOI

My poems appear somewhere
between my dreams and prose.

Swept up on a sandy shoal,
indecently exposed at low tide.

My poems wither in the sun
waiting to be devoured by

shrieking scavenger seagulls,
excreting guano on some deserted island,

washed clean in the rhyme and the rhythm
of the sea.

From whence dreams come, my poems,
inchoate, anonymous, will be recycled

forever, if we believe our world's
forever.

AFTERWORD

Topographies of Soul:
The Poetry of Henry Morgenthau III

A Sunday in Purgatory is the debut poetry collection of a celebrated writer of memoir, a former producer/pioneer of Public Television, and a first hand witness to some of the most gripping moments in twentieth-century American history. The poet came to his new craft at ninety-six years old and spent three years generating the book you hold in your hands. It is not so much a glance backwards as a look inward, his subjects including aging and mortality, the politics of identity, and the shape of wonder.

I first met Henry Morgenthau III when he signed up for a community poetry workshop I was teaching. It was the fall of 2012. Having spent his professional life documenting the work of legendary Americans ranging from Eleanor Roosevelt to Martin Luther King Jr., James Baldwin, and President Kennedy, having written a memoir, *Mostly Morgenthaus,* on the subject of his distinguished family – which includes his father, Henry Morgenthau Jr., who was Secretary of the Treasury under FDR, and grandfather, Henry Morgenthau, Ambassador to Turkey, whose struggle against the Armenian genocide there is well documented – Morgenthau III found in poetry a space in which to approach subjects untouchable in his earlier writing. In poetry there is a way in which a certain doubtfulness, a questioning spirit can be investigated. The title piece, "A Sunday in Purgatory," is among the first poems he wrote. It was published one year later in *Nimrod International Journal.* He got off to an auspicious start.

What draws me to Morgenthau's poetry is the tough-minded treatment of his subject matter, which is highly diverse. As in Lowell's *Life Studies,* the poet is writing a personal and national history that goes beyond dates and people and places, and which begins to map a topography of soul. His recollections of his White House years are gripping. In "A Marvelous Party" (its title taken from a Noel Coward song), Morgenthau describes a night on Cap d'Antibes in 1938, a party "for the future heroes and collaborationists basking/in the Mediterranean sun" during "our last summer" – last summer of youth (the poem is autobiographical); last summer of innocence (Hitler invades Poland on September 1, 1939). In attendance is Bea "Lady Peel," who will lose her son in the war. But this night, "she sings of a marvelous party." The song, separate from the marvelous party they're having, records emotional displacement so brilliantly. On the eve of war, on the eve of adulthood, the speaker attends this beautiful soirée but feels once removed from it. *"I couldn't have loved it more,*" the chanteuse sings, her wistfulness providing mood music for all of *A Sunday in Purgatory.* To be alive is to be in attendance of such a party. How difficult to be present for it, knowing the cost.

In the 1960s, while working on an early documentary for Public Television, Morgenthau interviewed the poet Robert Lowell. That meeting remained close at heart; Lowell's poetry has proved a central influence and constant companion over the years. One can hear Morgenthau's diction and cadences in these last lines from Lowell's "For the Union Dead":

> The Aquarium is gone. Everywhere,
> giant finned cars nose forward like fish;
> a savage servility
> slides by on grease.

The "savage servility" of life in town, in the same moment brutal and submissive, is a concoction of contradictions and dualities. In Lowell's poetry, and here, in Morgenthau's, we are both victim and torturer. The language of these lines embodies opposites, too, somewhat tribal, guttural, Anglo-Saxon ("*cars nose* forward like *fish*") and Latinate at others ("aquarium," "servility"). This tiny stanza encourages a cognitive dissonance at the level of language.

Poetry always demands a disturbance that ejects us from the known. It questions our sometimes too easy labeling of the other and the self. So it is in poetry that Morgenthau has found a space to confront, even unravel, his entanglements, or more: to just describe them as they are. In a central poem, "Ladyfingers," the speaker tells of a 1920s childhood in which roles within a powerful political and observant Jewish family were set firmly in place, creating a cocoon to protect him, as well as a cage to hold back the desires of the spirit and the body. Morgenthau writes:

> On the first day of classes,
> boys and girls were separated.
> The girls were handed
> pastel-colored chiffon scarves
> to wave as they gamboled about.
> I grabbed one, and followed the girls,
> prompting jeers from the boys.
> "Hey Ladyfingers," yelled Henry Furnald,
> the best looking boy in the class.
> "Hey Ladyfingers!"
> He was one of the boys. I was not.

The language is so reminiscent of Lowell. The so-called "high" and "low" diction, the necessary sonic dissonance that captures the emotions of the child: the girls "gamboled" waving "pastel-colored chiffon scarves," while the boys "jeer[ed]" (from Germanic *shear* and *scar*). In the poem the speaker is caught between his designated role – as a boy he was given no scarf – and his desire. At the heart of confessional poetry, Octavio Paz once said, is the impulse of the speaker not merely to blame the others with an accusing finger, but also to turn the finger on the self. In its very title, "Ladyfingers" does that. As much as the speaker lays blame on the world into which he was born, he also names himself complicit in the cocooning:

> I have lived with the dread of being uncovered.
> I have built walls to isolate myself,
> to hide behind, to fear, and to hate myself.
> Walls fabricated with stony
> indifference toward being different.
> Not wanting to be touched.
> Wanting to touch.

Morgenthau's poetry *does* finally make contact in the way he longs to, its images and ideas and extraordinary language evocative of what he calls "the soft, sensuous pressure of warm bath water." A confessional poet, his confession is one of great beauty, because it is an acknowledgment of seeing things merely as they are, without the need to be adjusted or fixed or revised in retrospect. *A Sunday in Purgatory* articulates human feelings – from the subtle and the complicated to the loud and clear – as well as any book of poetry I have read in years.

David Keplinger
Rome 2016

FURTHER ACKNOWLEDGMENTS

I want to thank all the people who worked with me to make this book possible. First and foremost, the two poets, David Keplinger and Bonnie Naradzay, whose encouragement, forthcoming with incredible generosity, gave me the courage to offer these poems for publication.

Thank you also to the good people at Passager Books, who worked patiently and tirelessly with me: the editors, Kendra Kopelke and Mary Azrael, the art director and graphic designer, Pantea Amin Tofangchi, and managing editor Christine Drawl.

And thank you to the Writers Center in Bethesda and to Politics and Prose in Washington, D.C. for offering excellent poetry workshops, and to Lynn Dizard, who has organized the poetry workshops and readings at Ingleside at Rock Creek.

A Sunday in Purgatory was designed and typeset by Pantea Amin Tofangchi using Adobe InDesign. The pages are set in Adobe Garamond Pro.

The cover art is a 36x48 acrylic painting by Steve Matanle titled "Fortune's Gate." A detail of the painting is used with his kind permission.

Printed in 2016 by Spencer Printing, Honesdale, PA.

In legends, the crane stands for longevity, peace, harmony, good fortune and fidelity. A high flyer, it is cherished for its ability to see both heaven and earth. These ancient, magnificent birds, so crucial in the wild as an "umbrella species," are now endangered and must be protected.

Passager Books is dedicated to making public the passions of a generation vital to our survival.

If you would like to support Passager Books, please visit our website www.passagerbooks.com or email us at editors@passagerbooks.com.

Also from Passager Books

A Cartography of Peace
Jean L. Connor

Improvise in the Amen Corner
Larnell Custis Butler

A Little Breast Music
Shirley J. Brewer

A Hinge of Joy
Jean L. Connor

Everything Is True at Once
Bart Galle

Perris, California
Norma Chapman

Nightbook
Steve Matanle

I Shall Go As I Came
Ellen Kirvin Dudis

Keeping Time:
150 Years of Journal Writing
edited by Mary Azrael and Kendra Kopelke

Burning Bright:
Passager Celebrates 21 Years
edited by Mary Azrael and Kendra Kopelke

Hot Flash Sonnets
Moira Egan

Beyond Lowu Bridge
Roy Cheng Tsung

Because There Is No Return
Diana Anhalt

Never the Loss of Wings
Maryhelen Snyder

The Want Fire
Jennifer Wallace

Little Miracles
James K. Zimmerman

View from the Hilltop
A Collection by The North Oaks Writers
edited by Barbara Sherr Roswell and Christine Drawl

The Chugalug King & Other Stories
Andrew Brown

Gathering the Soft
Becky Dennison Sakellariou
Paintings by Tandy Zorba

Finding Mr. Rightstein
Nancy Davidoff Kelton

The Three O'Clock Bird
Anne Frydman